Picture credits:

Pg17 l: Shutterstock/Ilona Ignatova; Pg18 r: Shutterstock/TonyV3112

Pg19 b: Shutterstock/Pigprox; Pg30 b: Shutterstock/Colette3

Pg35 t: iStock/RapidEye; Pg38 t: Shutterstock/ingehogenbijl

Pg 41 t: Shutterstock/Bertl123; Pg 42 t: Shutterstock/VanderWolf Images

Pg44 t: Shutterstock/Paul Daniels; Pg 44b: Shutterstock/Vibrant Image Studio

NASA/GSFC/METI/ERSDAC/JAROS and U.S./Japan ASTER Science Team:
pg 27 bottom right
Bjorn van der Velpen: pg 32 top
Tom Wiberg: pg 35 centre

U.S. Navy photo by Photographer's Mate 1st Class James Thierry: pg 36 bottom

Published 2017 by North Parade Publishing Ltd.
4 North Parade, Bath, England.

Printed in China

CONTENTS

SUPER STRUCTURES

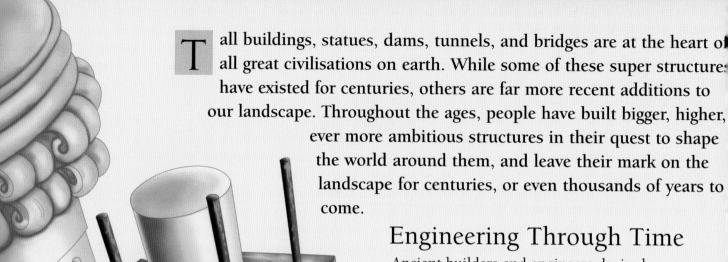

Tall buildings, statues, dams, tunnels, and bridges are at the heart of all great civilisations on earth. While some of these super structures have existed for centuries, others are far more recent additions to our landscape. Throughout the ages, people have built bigger, higher, ever more ambitious structures in their quest to shape the world around them, and leave their mark on the landscape for centuries, or even thousands of years to come.

Engineering Through Time

Ancient builders and engineers devised ingenious, creative ways to transport building materials to their construction sites. Their ability to design and build even the most simple structures is incredible when we consider the limited technology available to them. Today their constructions are regarded as some of the most beautiful, iconic landmarks in the world.

Ancient Greeks building the Parthenon. The Greeks used innovative construction methods that were very advanced for the time.

Ancient Techniques

Throughout history, civilisations have developed different techniques to build structures unique to the time and needs of their society. The Roman aqueducts and the Hanging Gardens of Babylon, for example, reveal a detailed understanding of engineering, and the ways in which it can be used to overcome geographical obstacles. Greek historian Strabo wrote in detail about how the Hanging Gardens were watered. Since there was very little rainfall in Babylon, the gardens had to be watered by the Euphrates River. Strabo describes how the water was lifted up to the garden in buckets attached to chain pumps. Turning wheels connected to the chain carried the water from the river to a pool at the top of the gardens, where it was released by gates into channels which acted as artificial streams.

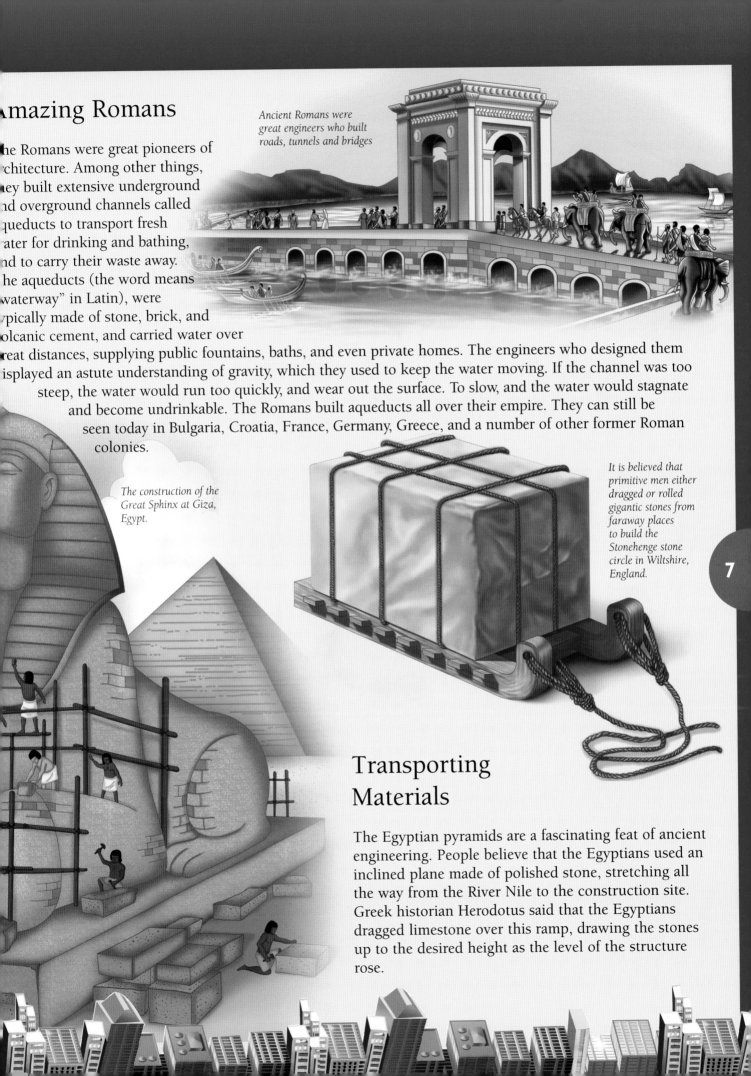

Amazing Romans

The Romans were great pioneers of architecture. Among other things, they built extensive underground and overground channels called aqueducts to transport fresh water for drinking and bathing, and to carry their waste away. The aqueducts (the word means "waterway" in Latin), were typically made of stone, brick, and volcanic cement, and carried water over great distances, supplying public fountains, baths, and even private homes. The engineers who designed them displayed an astute understanding of gravity, which they used to keep the water moving. If the channel was too steep, the water would run too quickly, and wear out the surface. To slow, and the water would stagnate and become undrinkable. The Romans built aqueducts all over their empire. They can still be seen today in Bulgaria, Croatia, France, Germany, Greece, and a number of other former Roman colonies.

Ancient Romans were great engineers who built roads, tunnels and bridges

The construction of the Great Sphinx at Giza, Egypt.

It is believed that primitive men either dragged or rolled gigantic stones from faraway places to build the Stonehenge stone circle in Wiltshire, England.

Transporting Materials

The Egyptian pyramids are a fascinating feat of ancient engineering. People believe that the Egyptians used an inclined plane made of polished stone, stretching all the way from the River Nile to the construction site. Greek historian Herodotus said that the Egyptians dragged limestone over this ramp, drawing the stones up to the desired height as the level of the structure rose.

7

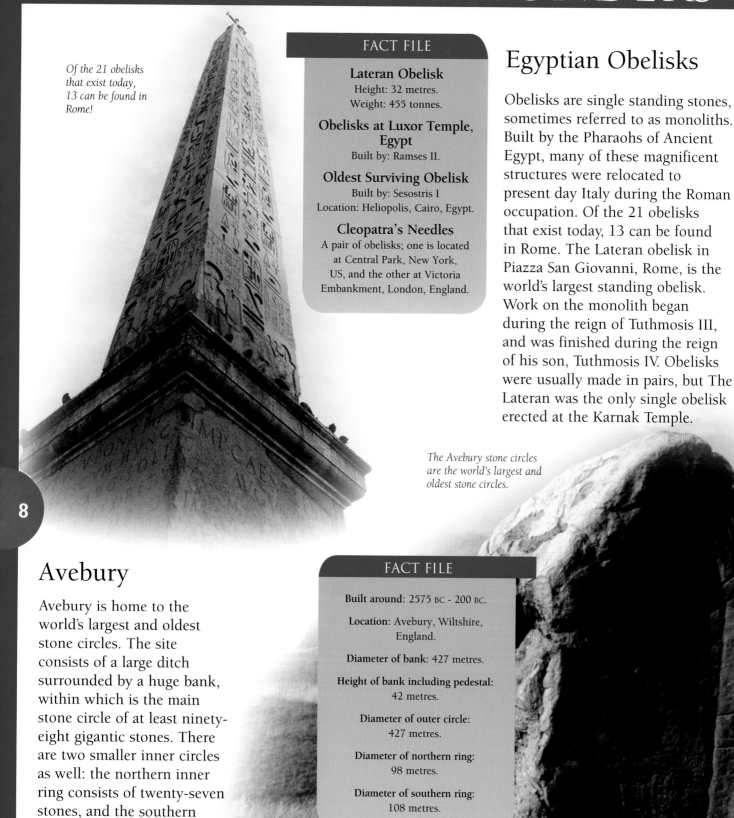

Of the 21 obelisks that exist today, 13 can be found in Rome!

FACT FILE

Lateran Obelisk
Height: 32 metres.
Weight: 455 tonnes.

Obelisks at Luxor Temple, Egypt
Built by: Ramses II.

Oldest Surviving Obelisk
Built by: Sesostris I
Location: Heliopolis, Cairo, Egypt.

Cleopatra's Needles
A pair of obelisks; one is located at Central Park, New York, US, and the other at Victoria Embankment, London, England.

Egyptian Obelisks

Obelisks are single standing stones, sometimes referred to as monoliths. Built by the Pharaohs of Ancient Egypt, many of these magnificent structures were relocated to present day Italy during the Roman occupation. Of the 21 obelisks that exist today, 13 can be found in Rome. The Lateran obelisk in Piazza San Giovanni, Rome, is the world's largest standing obelisk. Work on the monolith began during the reign of Tuthmosis III, and was finished during the reign of his son, Tuthmosis IV. Obelisks were usually made in pairs, but The Lateran was the only single obelisk erected at the Karnak Temple.

The Avebury stone circles are the world's largest and oldest stone circles.

8

Avebury

Avebury is home to the world's largest and oldest stone circles. The site consists of a large ditch surrounded by a huge bank, within which is the main stone circle of at least ninety-eight gigantic stones. There are two smaller inner circles as well: the northern inner ring consists of twenty-seven stones, and the southern inner ring twenty-nine. The original purpose and meaning of the stones remains a mystery.

FACT FILE

Built around: 2575 BC - 200 BC.

Location: Avebury, Wiltshire, England.

Diameter of bank: 427 metres.

Height of bank including pedestal: 42 metres.

Diameter of outer circle: 427 metres.

Diameter of northern ring: 98 metres.

Diameter of southern ring: 108 metres.

Pyramids of Giza

The largest of Giza's pyramids was built as a tomb for the pharaoh Khufu, and for almost 4,000 years it remained the tallest structure in the world! Of the Seven Wonders of the Ancient World, the Great Pyramid is the only one that still stands today. The other two pyramids are those of Khufu's son, Khafre, and of his grandson, Menkaure. The Great Sphinx, with a human head and a lion's body, is situated south of the Great Pyramid.

Like Stonehenge, the Avebury Stone Circles have several legends attached to them. According to one, the structure was built by aliens. Some people believe that the stones at Avebury are similar to the Cydonia stones found on Mars, and are even arranged in the same pattern!

FACT FILE

Pyramid of Giza

Built: *c.* 2575-2566 BC.

Number of stones: around 2.3 million blocks.

Height: originally around 147 metres.

Great Sphinx

Length: 73 metres.

Height: 20 metres.

The Great Pyramid of Giza was the tallest structure in the world for over 3,800 years!

9

Sphinx of Las Vegas

The Luxor Hotel in Las Vegas, US, was designed and constructed to replicate the Great Pyramid of Giza. The 30-storey hotel has over 4,000 rooms and is made entirely of black glass. The tip of the pyramid contains a spotlight that is said to be the brightest in the world. Guarding this extraordinarily modern building is a Sphinx that is almost twice the size of the original. The pyramid also features a reproduction of the Egyptian pharaoh Tutankhamun's tomb. Construction of the hotel began in 1991. It was opened on October 15, 1993.

The Sphinx outside the Luxor Hotel in Las Vegas.

Great Wall of China

The Great Wall of China was built over a period of two centuries. The structure was originally three separate walls used to protec the independent states of Yan, Zhao, and Qi from invasion. The First Emperor of China, Shi Huangdi of the Qin dynasty, unified thes separate state walls in an attempt to protect his country from the Huns. The wall was later reconstructed by succeeding dynasties. The structure we see today is the work of the Ming dynasty.

FACT FILE

Built in its modern form between the 14th and 16th centuries.

Extends up to: 6,700 kilometres.

Dynasties responsible for the construction: Qin, Han and Ming, as well as a few other short-lived dynasties.

Average height: 7-8 m (23-26 feet).

The wall as we see today was largely reconstructed by the Ming dynasty.

10

Hanging Gardens of Babylon

It is believed that the Babylonian king Nebuchadnezzar II built the Hanging Gardens for his wife, Amytis, who was homesick for the green, mountainous terrain of her homeland in the Median Empire. In order to please his wife, the king ordered the construction of the celebrated tiered gardens containing all manner of trees, shrubs, and vines. Romantic as the story may be, today's historians believe the Hanging Gardens might never have existed, except in the imagination of Greek intellectuals like Strabo.

The legendary Hanging Gardens of Babylon.

FACT FILE

Built by: Nebuchadnezzar II.

Date of construction: *c.* 605 BC.

Height: Believed to have been over 25 metres.

Length: 122 metres according to the Greek historian Siculus.

Width: 122 metres according to Siculus.

Materials used: Bricks, asphalt, stone slabs, and sheets of lead.

An ancient Roman aqueduct in France

FACT FILE

Famous Roman Aqueducts
Estimated lengths:

Aqua Virgo: 21 km (13 miles).

Aqua Claudia: 70 km (43 miles).

Aqua Marcia: 91 km (57 miles).

Anio Novus: 87 km (54 miles).

Aqua Appia: 16 km (10 miles).

One of the legends surrounding the Great Wall relates to young Meng Jiangnu, whose husband, Fan Qiliang, was forced to work on building the wall by the emperor's officials. Arriving at the site in search of her husband, Jiangnu was informed of Qiliang's death. Heart-broken, Jiangnu started to cry so hard that a huge part of the wall collapsed!

Roman Aqueducts

Ancient Roman aqueducts carried water over large distances, sometimes over 90 kilometres! Water from higher altitudes – such as that from mountain springs – was carried down to the city through underground tunnels. Wherever the ground level dipped, walls or arches had to be built to maintain the water level and pressure. When it reached the city, the water was stored in a large tank called a "castellum", and from there was distributed to public fountains and baths via network of smaller pipes, or "castella".

11

California Aqueduct

Aqueducts are still used today in several parts of the world - a few of the original Roman ones are still partially in use! One of the finest examples of a modern aqueduct is one located in California, running from the Sacramento River Delta to Lake Perris in Riverside County on the one hand, to Castaic Lake in Angeles National Forest on the other. Although the Roman aqueducts are arguably more beautiful, this 444-mile aqueduct in California is the longest in the world!

The Californian Aqueduct averages a width of 12 metres and a depth of 9 metres.

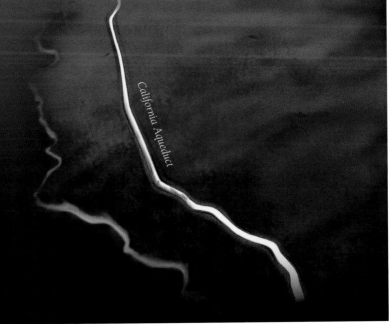

California Aqueduct

Ziggurats

Ziggurats were huge structures built in the Mesopotamian valley and western Iranian plateau. These terraced step pyramids were topped with a shrine, and were believed to bring people both physically and spititually closer to God. Perhaps the most famous surviving ziggurat is the Great Ziggurat of Ur, built in the Early Bronze Age (21st century BC) in honour of the moon god, Sin.

FACT FILE

Location: Nasiriyah, in the present-day Dhi Qar Province, Iraq (previously the city of Ur).

Built by: King Ur-Nammu.

Construction: c. 21st century BC.

Height: 30 metres (estimated as only foundations survive).

A Ziggurat in Chichen Itza, Yucatan, Mexico

Lighthouse of Alexandria

Of all the Seven Wonders of the Ancient World, the Lighthouse of Alexandria was the only one to be put to practical use. Sometimes called the Pharos of Alexandira after the island it was built upon, the lighthouse was comissioned by the ruler of Egypt, Ptolemy I Soter, in the 3rd century BC. The structure took twelve years to complete, and was finished during the reign of Ptolemy's son, Ptolemy II Philadelphus. It was a remarkable feat of engineering, serving as a prototype for all the other lighthouses that followed.

FACT FILE

Built by : Ptolemy I Soter; completed by Ptolemy II Philadelphus.

Construction: c. 280 BC.

Architect: Sostratus of Cnidus.

Estimated height: 134 metres.

Destroyed by: Earthquakes in 956, 1303 and 1323.

Colossus of Rhodes

The Colossus of Rhodes was a giant statue of the ancient Greek titan-god of the sun, Helios. It was built to celebrate the Rhodian victory over the ruler of Cyprus, whose son unsuccessfully besieged Rhodes in 305 BC. Before its destruction in the earthquake of 226 BC, the Colossus stood over 30 metres high, making it one of the tallest statues of the ancient world. Thousands of years after its destruction, this remarkable symbol of freedom and unity influenced the construction of another: the Statue of Liberty, completed in 1886, bears striking architectural similarities to the Colossus, the lost, but not forgotten wonder of the ancient world, which stood for just 54 years.

The Colossus of Rhodes stood guard at the harbour of the ancient Greek city for 56 years.

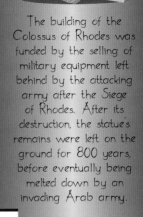

The building of the Colossus of Rhodes was funded by the selling of military equipment left behind by the attacking army after the Siege of Rhodes. After its destruction, the statue's remains were left on the ground for 800 years, before eventually being melted down by an invading Arab army.

FACT FILE

Location: Present-day Mandraki Harbour, Rhodes, Greece.

Architect: Chares of Lindos.

Constructed over: 12 years.

Made of: Iron and bronze; marble pedestal.

Height: Over 32 metres.

Height of pedestal: 15 metres.

13

The Eiffel Tower

Built by engineer and architect Gustave Eiffel to mark the 100th anniversary of the French Revolution, the Eiffel Tower was originally only intended to last just 20 years. Today the structure is recognised all over the world as a symbol of France, and has welcomed almost 250 million visitors since its opening in 1889.

FACT FILE

Location: Paris, France

Height: 324 m

Completed: 1889

Since ancient times, humans have sought to shape the landscape around them, leaving their mark on the world for future generations to admire and enjoy. From skyscrapers and dams, to tunnels and bridges, today we are building more ambitious structures than ever before. With the aid of modern technology, this has become easier than ever. Cranes, excavators, and bulldozers have allowed us to reach new heights of architectural possibility.

Rising in Style

Although the term 'skyscraper' is relatively new, tall structures have been around for several hundred years. Over time, castle towers, pyramids, lighthouses, and cathedral buttresses gave way to the 100-storied skyscrapers of the modern world. The industrial revolution, which began in the 18th century, witnessed the use of new building materials like iron and steel. Most modern skyscrapers have a steel-and-concrete framework that works to strengthen the building, whilst at the same time keeping it lightweight.

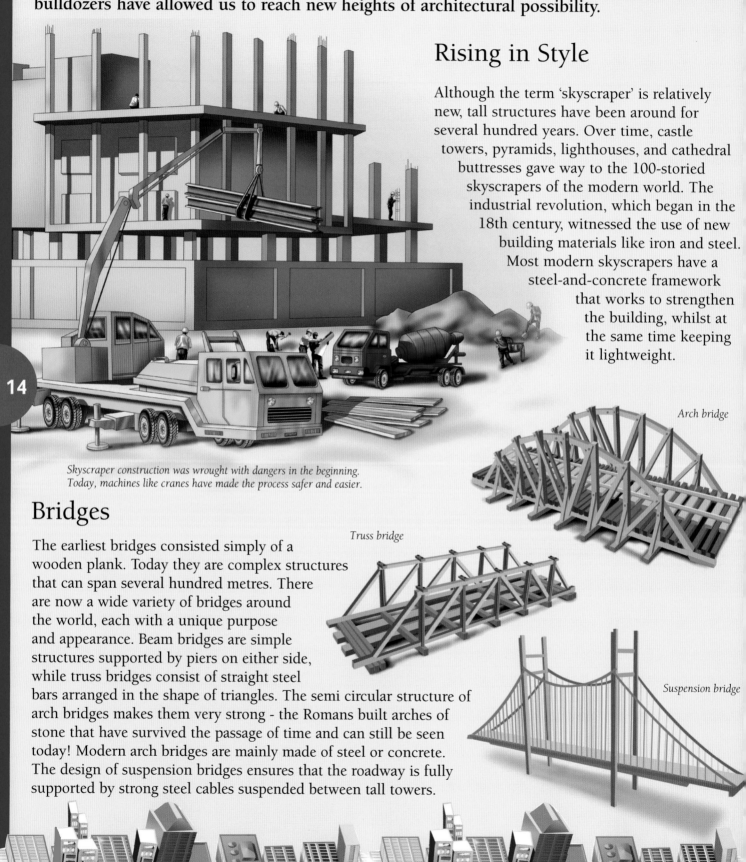

14

Skyscraper construction was wrought with dangers in the beginning. Today, machines like cranes have made the process safer and easier.

Arch bridge

Truss bridge

Suspension bridge

Bridges

The earliest bridges consisted simply of a wooden plank. Today they are complex structures that can span several hundred metres. There are now a wide variety of bridges around the world, each with a unique purpose and appearance. Beam bridges are simple structures supported by piers on either side, while truss bridges consist of straight steel bars arranged in the shape of triangles. The semi circular structure of arch bridges makes them very strong - the Romans built arches of stone that have survived the passage of time and can still be seen today! Modern arch bridges are mainly made of steel or concrete. The design of suspension bridges ensures that the roadway is fully supported by strong steel cables suspended between tall towers.

Tunnels

Tunnels were orginally used as secret passages. In Rome they were used to transport water over great distances. Today, however, tunnels provide alternative, space-efficient routes for transportation. The basic elements of tunnel construction include digging through the earth and lining the tunnel with strong materials. Underwater tunnels are especially difficult to build. Engineers must use pressurised digging chambers to prevent flooding. Today it is common to construct parts of the tunnel on land rather than assembling it all underwater.

While digging a tunnel, engineers must ensure that the area around it is well supported to prevent it from caving in.

Dams

Like so many other structures, dams have become an integral part of our lives. These enormous, useful constructions not only prevent flooding, but also store water for irrigation and producing electricity. Arch dams are usually built in narrow, rocky regions. Their curved shape forces the water pressure to act against the arches, strengthening the structure as it is pushed deeper into its foundations. Buttress dams are made of reinforced concrete, and held in place by a series of supports. Embankment dams are heavy, and made of earth and rock. They have a waterproof core that prevents water from entering the structure, and the weight of the dam itself acts as a barrier against the force of the water. Huge dams that hold back water through their weight alone are called gravity dams. They are made from millions of tonnes of concrete, and are therefore very expensive to build.

Dams have to be extraordinarily strong to withstand the pressures of a raging river.

TOWERING TALL

FACT FILE

Location:
Dubai, United Arab Emirates.

Height: 829.8 metres.

Architect: Adrian Smith.

Construction began: January 2004.

Opened: 2010.

Burj Khalifa

The height of this extraordinary structure seems to defy the very laws of physics! This megatall superstructure is supported by a large reinforced concrete mat, which is in turn supported by bored reinforced concrete piles. Adorned with over 1,000 pieces of art, the Burj Khalifa has become a cultural centre point of Dubai, having been used several times for firework displays in the city. There are even plans to extend it even farther upwards!

FACT FILE

Location:
Xinyi district, Taipei, Taiwan.

Height: 508 m (1,667 feet).

Architects:
C.Y. Lee & Partners.

Construction began:
June 1999.

Opened on:
December 31, 2004.

Located in an earthquake-prone zone, Taipei 101 is claimed to be capable of withstanding even the strongest tremors.

Taipei 101

The Taipei Financial Centre, popularly known as Taipei 101, was the world's tallest building until 2010. It has 101 storeys, but that does not mean it takes ages to reach the top of the tower - this engineering marvel boasts the fastest elevators in the world! Travelling at speeds of up to 60 km/h, these elevators can reach the very top of the building in around 40 seconds! Taipei 101 is designed to withstand the earthquakes that are common in this part of the world, and is home to the largest damper sphere in existence. This 660 tonne steel pendulum, suspended from the 92nd to the 87th floors, sways in order to offset movements in the building caused by strong gusts.

The Petronas Towers featured in the 1999 film, Entraptment, featurig Sean Connery and Catherine Zeta-Jones.

Petronas Towers

The Petronas Towers were the world's tallest buildings until they were overtaken by Taipei 101, which overshot them by an astonishing 56 metres! The geometric design of the towers was inspired by traditional Islamic patterns. The design plan is that of an eight-pointed star, with circular arcs in the inner angles. This pattern symbolises unity, harmony, and stability. Each tower is 88 storeys high and has a total of over 30,000 windows! Another unique feature of this architectural wonder is the 58-metre-long double-deck skybridge which connects the twin structures.

Alain 'Spiderman' Robert, a rock climber from France, has a unique occupation: he climbs skyscrapers! This real-life Spiderman has climbed tall buildings like the Sears Tower with his bare hands, and without any safety net. In a span of eight years, Alain has scaled more than 70 skyscrapers and monuments!

FACT FILE

Location: Kuala Lumpur, Malaysia.

Height: 452 metres.

Architects: Cesar Pelli & Associates.

Construction began: 1993.

Opened: August 28, 1999.

Apart from the Freedom Tower, the rebuilding plan for the World Trade Center includes four other office. towers.

One World Trade Centre

The twin towers of the World Trade Center in New York, destroyed in the terrorist attacks of September 2001, were commemorated in 2014 with the completion of the Freedom Tower. This beautiful building is is 541.4 metres (1,776 feet) tall, including an 84-metre (276 foot) spire. The height of 1,776 feet was chosen to commemorate the year the United States of America declared its independence from Britain. The tower's design was proposed by Daniel Libeskind, an architect from Berlin. As well as the Freedom Tower itself, the rebuilding plan also includes four other office towers and a memorial to the victims of the terrorist attacks. In 2009, the Freedom Tower was renamed One World Trade Centre.

Burj al Arab

The Burj al Arab is the world's tallest structure to be used exclusively as an hotel. But that is not the only thing that makes this building unique. Located in the United Arab Emirates, the hotel is constructed on a man-made island around 280 metres from the coastline. Shaped like a giant sail, the Burj al Arab has been built in such a way that its shadow does not fall on the beach nearby. The 60-storey hotel consists of over 200 duplex suites and even has a helipad on its roof!

FACT FILE

Location: Jumeirah Beach Road, Dubai, United Arab Emirates.

Height: 321 metres.

Height of atrium: 182 metres.

Architects: WS Atkins & Partners.

Construction began: 1994.

Opened: December 1, 1999.

The Burj al Arab has been built in such a way that its shadow does not fall on the beach nearby.

Shanghai Tower

Standing tall at an astounding 632 metres, the Shanghai Tower is currently China's tallest structure. Despite being completed in September 2015, the Tower was not fully open to visitors until March 2016. It comprises the world's first adjacent grouping of three supertall buildings, another of which is the Jin Mao Tower. At the time of completion, the Shanghai Tower housed the second highest hotel in the world. The building is designed as nine cylindrical structures placed on top of one another and will eventually house a museum!

The construction of the Shanghai Tower used a lot of Green Architecture, with the building's heating and cooling systems using geothermal energy.

FACT FILE

Location: Pudong district, Shanghai, People's Republic of China.

Height: 632 metres.

Architect: Jun Xia.

Construction began: 2008.

Completed: 2015.

Opened: 2016.

FACT FILE

Location: Manhattan, New York City, U.S.

Height: 381 metres.

Architects: Shreve, Lamb & Harmon Associates.

Construction began: 1930.

Opened: May 1, 1931.

The grand opening of the Empire State Building on May 1, 1931 began with a traditional ribbon cutting ceremony, followed by a switching on of the skyscraper's lights. But President Hoover, who lit up the building, didn't come to New York for the event. At home in Washington, D.C., Hoover pressed a button signalling the instantaneous activation of the building's electric illumination system some 200 miles away!

Empire State Building

Before the construction of the World Trade Center, the Empire State Building was the tallest building in New York City. Completed in a record time (a little over a year!), it surpassed the Chrysler Building to become world's tallest building. Regarded as one of the Seven Wonders of the modern world, the Empire State Building houses several television broadcasting stations on its topmost levels.

The Empire State Building is struck by lightning around a hundred times a year! Fortunately, it is designed to withstand such events.

19

The primary role of the Tokyo Skytree is the transmission of digital terrestrial broadcasting.

Tokyo Skytree

At 634 metres high, the Tokyo Skytree is now the tallest freestanding tower in the world, overtaking the Canton Tower which held the top spot for just two years. The design of the Tokyo Skytree fuses modern and traditional Japanese architecture to reflect the history and culture of the land it surveys.

Euro Tunnel

The Euro Tunnel comprises two main rail tunnels beneath the English Channel.

Attempts to link France and England date as far back as 1880. However, the British Prime Minister of the time, William Gladstone, abandoned the idea on grounds of national security. It was felt that a tunnel would provide easy access for France, and encourage an invasion. After many years, the idea was revived in the form of the Eurotunnel – one of the longest rail tunnels in the world. It consists of two main rail tunnels beneath the English Channel, with a service tunnel in between.

FACT FILE

Connects: Cheritan, Kent, England, and Sangatte, northern France.

Total length:
50 km (30 miles)

Length underwater:
39 km (24 miles)

Construction began:
1988.

Completed:
1994.

Seikan Tunnel

It all started with a tragedy. Until the Seikan Tunnel was built, the only way to cross the Tsugaru Strait in Japan was by ferry. Disaster struck in 1954, when five ferries sank during a typhoon, killing 1,430 passengers. At last the government began to consider safer alternatives. Since bridges were equally hazardous due to the wild weather, engineers proposed an underwater tunnel instead. Building the Seikan Tunnel was difficult and dangerous - 34 workers died during the construction. The volcanic rock beneath the strait was so unstable that tunnel-boring machines could not be used, and workers had to blast through the rock instead.

FACT FILE

Seikan Tunnel

Connects: the Japanese Islands of Honshu and Hokkaido.

Total length: 53.8 km.

Length underwater: 23.3 km.

Construction began: 1964.

Completed: 1988.

The special lighting in the Laerdal Tunnel is aimed at keeping drivers awake, thus preventing accidents.

The world's longest and deepest rail tunnel opened in Switzerland in June 2016, surpassing the previous record holder, the Seikan Tunnel in Japan. The Gotthard rail link took 20 years to build and, the Swiss say, will revolutionise Europe's freight transport.

Laerdal Tunnel

The world's longest road tunnel, the Laerdal Tunnel in Norway, cuts through an Alpine mountain range. The tunnel provides a shorter route between the cities of Bergen and Oslo, and is also a safer alternative to the long and narrow route up the mountains. The Laerdal Tunnel is regarded as one of the world's safest tunnels. One of its unique features includes the three mountain caverns or 'halls', designed to allow vehicles to turn back in case of fire at the other end. Alarm systems have also been installed to warn of danger.

FACT FILE

Laerdal Tunnel
Connects: Laerdal and Aurland in western Norway.

Total length: 24.5 km.

Construction began: 1995.

Completed: 2000.

Inaugurated:
November 27, 2000.

Thames Tunnel

The world's first underwater tunnel, the Thames Tunnel, was completed 1825. Prior to this, all attempts to dig a tunnel beneath the River Thames had failed miserably. The turning point came in 1823, when French engineer, Marc Isambard Brunel created the tunnelling shield, a revolutionary advance in tunnelling technology. At last workers were able to tunnel through soil too soft or fluid to remain stable while they lined the perimeter with concrete, cast iron, or steel. In effect, the shield served as a temporary support structure for the tunnel while it was being excavated.

The world's first underwater tunnel was finally completed in 1843, twenty years after Brunel's revolutionary idea.
The Thames Tunnel, originally built for carriages, was converted to a railway tunnel in 1865, and became a part of the London Underground in 1913.

The Thames Tunnel was originally built for carriages, but was converted into a railway tunnel in 1865.

MEGA BRIDGES

FACT FILE

Connects: Tsing Yi and Ma Wan islands, Hong Kong.

Construction began: May 1992.

Completed: May 1997.

Height: 206 metres.

Tsing Ma

The Tsing Ma Bridge, named after the two islands it connects (Tsing Yi and Ma Wan) is the world's longest double-deck suspension bridge for both cars and trains. The centre of the bridge spans 1,377 metres across the Ma Wan Channel. The upper level of the bridge has six lanes for vehicles, while two rail tracks form the lower level. The bridge is a part of the Lantau Link, which connects the New Territories with the island of Chek Lap Kok, home to Hong Kong International Airport.

The Tsing Ma stretches between the islands of Tsing Yi and Ma Wan.

FACT FILE

Connects: Kobe and Awaji-shima, Japan.

Construction began: May 1988.

Completed: 1998.

Length of central span: 1,991 metres.

Height: 283 metres.

Akashi ▶ Kaikyo

Akashi Kaikyo

Golden Gate Bridge

Brooklyn Bridge

A comparison of the world's longest suspension bridge, the Akashi Kaikyo in Japan, with other suspension bridges.

The Akashi Kaikyo Bridge has the longest central span of any suspension bridge in the world. Originally intended to serve both rail and road traffic, by the time construction began in April 1988 it was decided to restrict the bridge to road vehicles only. The two towers were originally built 1,990 metres apart, but the Great Hanshin earthquake in January 1995, moved them so much that the span had to be increased by a metre! The bridge was designed with a two hinged stiffening girder system, enabling the structure to withstand rough winds, earthquakes, and harsh sea currents.

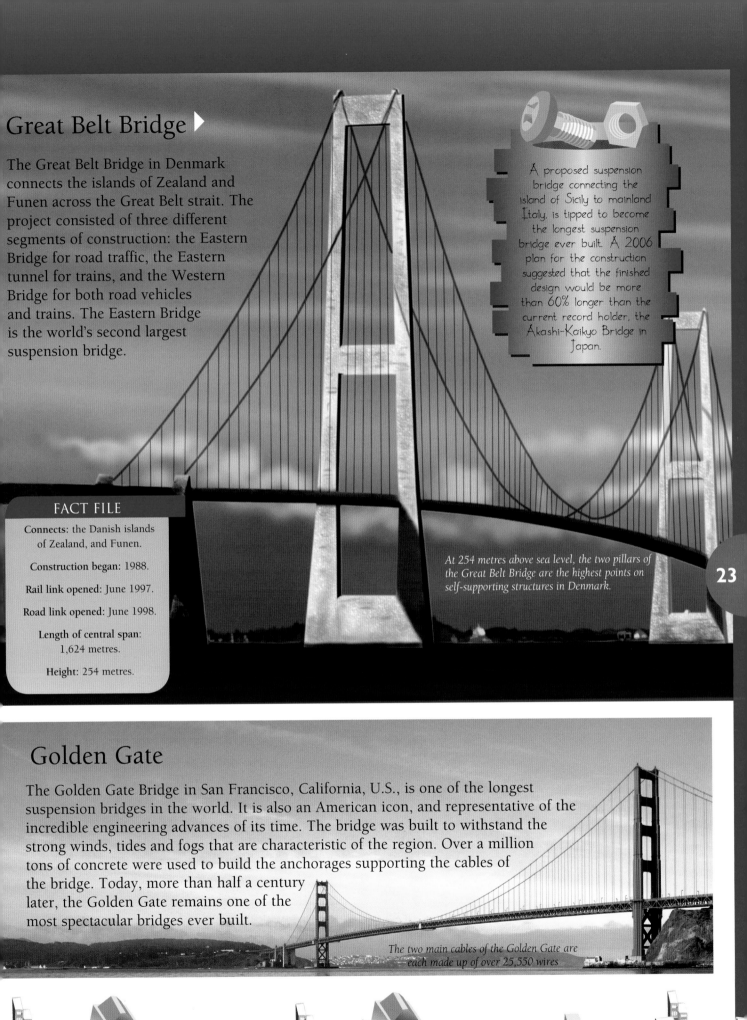

Great Belt Bridge ▶

The Great Belt Bridge in Denmark connects the islands of Zealand and Funen across the Great Belt strait. The project consisted of three different segments of construction: the Eastern Bridge for road traffic, the Eastern tunnel for trains, and the Western Bridge for both road vehicles and trains. The Eastern Bridge is the world's second largest suspension bridge.

A proposed suspension bridge connecting the island of Sicily to mainland Italy, is tipped to become the longest suspension bridge ever built. A 2006 plan for the construction suggested that the finished design would be more than 60% longer than the current record holder, the Akashi-Kaikyo Bridge in Japan.

FACT FILE

Connects: the Danish islands of Zealand, and Funen.

Construction began: 1988.

Rail link opened: June 1997.

Road link opened: June 1998.

Length of central span: 1,624 metres.

Height: 254 metres.

At 254 metres above sea level, the two pillars of the Great Belt Bridge are the highest points on self-supporting structures in Denmark.

Golden Gate

The Golden Gate Bridge in San Francisco, California, U.S., is one of the longest suspension bridges in the world. It is also an American icon, and representative of the incredible engineering advances of its time. The bridge was built to withstand the strong winds, tides and fogs that are characteristic of the region. Over a million tons of concrete were used to build the anchorages supporting the cables of the bridge. Today, more than half a century later, the Golden Gate remains one of the most spectacular bridges ever built.

The two main cables of the Golden Gate are each made up of over 25,550 wires

Lake Pontchartrain Causeway

The Lake Pontchartrain Causeway is the world's longest bridge over continuous water. The Causeway is composed of two parallel bridges, each about 38 kilometres long, connecting Mandeville and Metairie in Louisiana, U.S. The concrete used to build the bridge was precast and transported to construction points on the lake using barges. The bridge was then assembled on-site.

The Pontchartrain Causeway bridges are supported by 9,500 hollow pilings.

24

Lupu Bridge ▲

The Lupu Bridge in Shanghai, China, is the world's second longest steel-arch bridge, after the Chaotianmen Bridge in Chongqing. The arch of the Lupu Bridge is made up of 27 segments, stretching across the Huangpu River in Shanghai and connecting the city's Luwan and Pudong districts.

More than 60,000 vehicles pass over the Lupu Bridge every day.

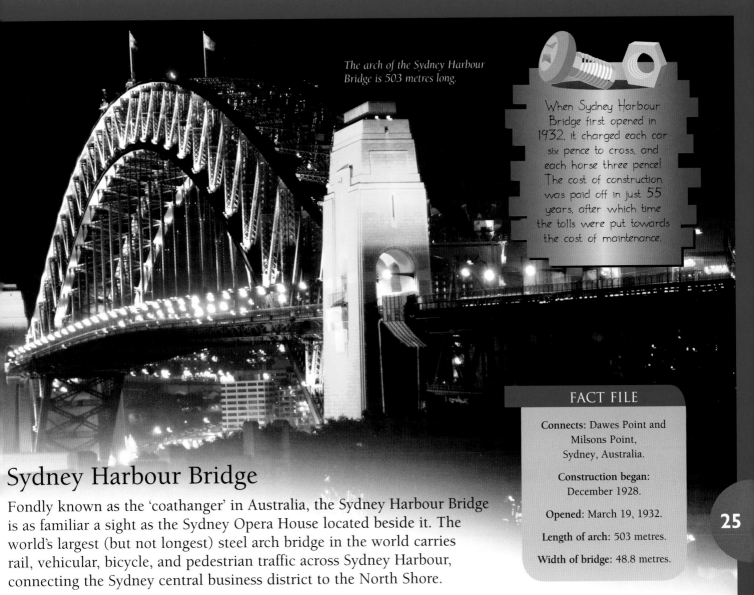

The arch of the Sydney Harbour Bridge is 503 metres long.

When Sydney Harbour Bridge first opened in 1932, it charged each car six pence to cross, and each horse three pence! The cost of construction was paid off in just 55 years, after which time the tolls were put towards the cost of maintenance.

Sydney Harbour Bridge

Fondly known as the 'coathanger' in Australia, the Sydney Harbour Bridge is as familiar a sight as the Sydney Opera House located beside it. The world's largest (but not longest) steel arch bridge in the world carries rail, vehicular, bicycle, and pedestrian traffic across Sydney Harbour, connecting the Sydney central business district to the North Shore.

FACT FILE

Connects: Dawes Point and Milsons Point, Sydney, Australia.

Construction began: December 1928.

Opened: March 19, 1932.

Length of arch: 503 metres.

Width of bridge: 48.8 metres.

Tower Bridge

The rapid expansion of London in the 19th century led to the requirement of an additional river crossing besides the famous London Bridge. In 1876, a Special Bridge or Subway Committee was formed for the purpose. The result was Tower Bridge. Designed by Sir Horace Jones, the bridge eased road traffic while maintaining river access to the busy Pool of London docks. With giant moveable roadways that lift up for passing ships, London Bridge is, to this day, considered an engineering marvel. As well as being one of London's favourite icons, it is arguably one of the most famous, and instantly recognisable structures in the world.

When it was built, Tower Bridge was the largest and most sophisticated bascule bridge in the world ("bascule" comes from the French word for "see-saw").

MEGA DAMS

The Hoover Dam is a concrete arch-gravity dam.

Hoover Dam

Hoover Dam, once known as Boulder Dam, is a concrete arch-gravity dam in the Black Canyon of the Colorado River. Situated on the border between the U.S. states of Nevada and Arizona, the dam was constructed between 1931 and 1936, during the Great Depression. Its construction was a tremendous effort, involving thousands of workers, and costing over one hundred lives. The dam was finally opened in 1936, and named after Herbert Hoover, President of the United States from 1929-1933.

FACT FILE

Located on: Arizona-Nevada border, U.S.

Construction began: April 20, 1931.

Completed: March 1, 1936.

Uses: Hydroelectric power, flood control, irrigation.

Reservoir: Lake Mead.

Materials used: Concrete.

Height: 221 metres.

Crest length: 379 metres.

Grand Coulee Dam

26

The Grand Coulee Dam is a gravity dam on the Columbia River in the U.S. state of Washington. It is the largest electric power-producing facility in the United States, and one of largest hydroelectric dams in the world. It was constructed between 1933 and 1942, originally with two power plants. Power from the dam fuelled the growing industries of Northwest United States throughout World War II, leading to the completion of a third power station in 1974 to help meet increasing energy demands.

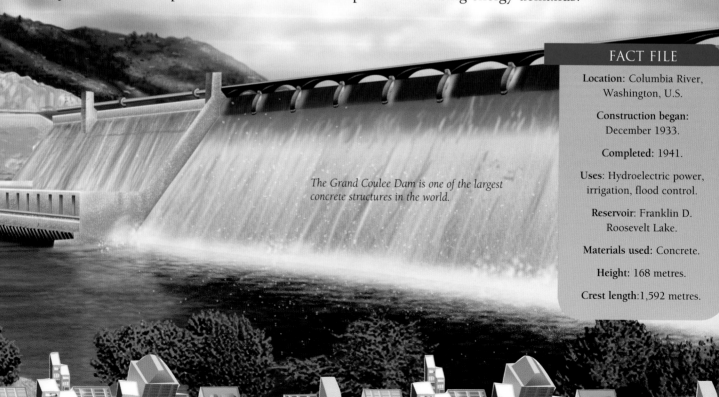

The Grand Coulee Dam is one of the largest concrete structures in the world.

FACT FILE

Location: Columbia River, Washington, U.S.

Construction began: December 1933.

Completed: 1941.

Uses: Hydroelectric power, irrigation, flood control.

Reservoir: Franklin D. Roosevelt Lake.

Materials used: Concrete.

Height: 168 metres.

Crest length: 1,592 metres.

The Itaipú Dam power plant consists of 18 generator units.

FACT FILE

Located in:
Brazil-Paraguay border.

Construction began: 1975.

Completed: 1991.

Uses: Hydroelectric power production.

Reservoir: Itaipú Reservoir.

Materials used: Concrete.

Height: 196 metres (643 feet).

Length: 7.7 km (4.8 miles).

Every summer, the Nile River flooded its banks leaving behind black soil suitable for agriculture. In 1970, the Aswan High Dam was built to control the river's annual flooding, so that farmers could plant crops throughout the year. Unfortunately, the dam has also prevented rich soil from being deposited on the riverbanks.

Itaipú Dam

The Itaipú Dam is one of the most expensive structures ever built. Around forty thousand people worked on the construction, using enough iron and steel to construct 380 Eiffel Towers! The final structure diverted the course of the seventh largest river in the world, shifting an astonishing 50 million tonnes of earth and rock in the process.

Three Gorges Dam

The Three Gorges Dam is a hydroelectric dam that spans the Yangtze River, beside the town of Sandouping, in the Hubei province of China. It is the world's largest power station in terms of installed capacity (22,500 MW).

In 2014, the dam generated 98.8 TWh of electricity, surpassing the Itaipú Dam and setting a new world record, but in 2015, the Itaipu power plant resumed the lead in annual worldwide production.

As well as producing electricity, the Three Gorges Dam is intended to increase the Yangtze River's shipping capacity and reduce the potential for floods downstream by providing flood storage space. The Chinese government regards the project as a historic engineering, social, and economic success story.

The reservoir of the Three Gorges Dam will submerge two of the three gorges.

Maracaña Stadium

It all began with the 1950 Fédération Internationale de Football Association (FIFA) World Cup. Brazil was chosen to host the prestigious event, and, to mark the occasion, commissioned the construction of a gigantic stadium – the like of which the world had never seen before. The result was the Maracaña stadium. Regarded as one of the world's largest football stadia, the Maracaña could once hold nearly 200,000 spectators! The introduction of new safety measures in the 1990s reduced the capacity of the stadium, and later redevelopment works involved the complete rebuilding of the bottom tier and the installation of a new roof. The stadium reopened 2nd June 2013, with a friendly international between Brazil and England (2-2), and today holds 79,000 spectators.

FACT FILE

Location: Rio de Janeiro, Brazil.

Construction began: 1948.

First match: June 16, 1950.

Estimated capacity: 200,000.

Maximum attendance: 199,854 - July 16, 1950, Brazil vs Uruguay World Cup Final.

Current capacity: 70,000-80,000; all-seater.

The stadium was officially renamed Estádio Mário Filho in 1966, following the dea[...] Brazilian journalist Mário Filho, but most people have continued to use the old nam[...]

May Day Stadium

The Rungrado May Day Stadium in Pyongyang, North Korea, was completed 1 May, 1989, and is the largest stadium in the world in terms of capacity. Originally constructed for the 13th World Festival of Youth and Students, the stadium has a capacity of 150,000. Although it is used as a sporting venue, it is most famous as the site of the annual Mass Games, a massive gymnastic and sporting event featuring over 100,000 participants.

FACT FILE

Location: Rungra Island, Taedong River, Pyongyang, North Korea.

Construction began: 1986.

Opened: May 1, 1989.

Capacity: 150,000; all seater.

The 16 arch roofs of the Mayday Stadium link together like the petals of a flower.

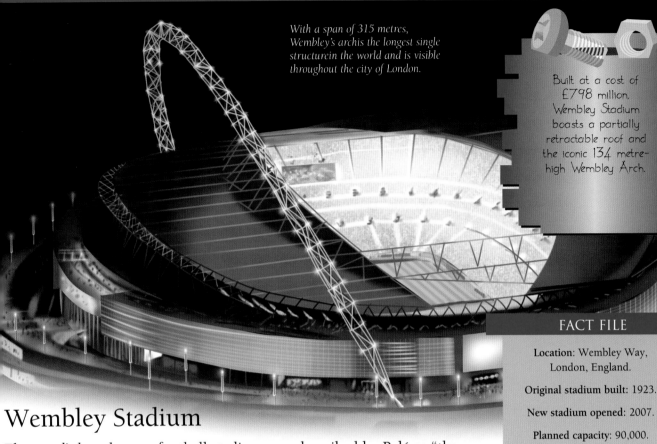

With a span of 315 metres, Wembley's arch is the longest single structure in the world and is visible throughout the city of London.

Built at a cost of £798 million, Wembley Stadium boasts a partially retractable roof and the iconic 134 metre-high Wembley Arch.

Wembley Stadium

The word's best-known football stadium was described by Pelé as "the cathedral of football. It is the capital of football and it is the heart of football". It was at Wembley that England won its first and only Football World Cup, in 1966. The original structure, first known as the Empire Stadium, opened in April 1923, but closed 77 years later in 2000 to be replaced in 2007 by New Wembley. With 90,000 seats, New Wembley is the largest stadium in the United Kingdom and the second-largest in Europe.

FACT FILE

Location: Wembley Way, London, England.

Original stadium built: 1923.

New stadium opened: 2007.

Planned capacity: 90,000.

Span of roof: 315 metres.

Height of the arch: 133 metres.

Tenants: England national football team (2007–present). Tottenham Hotspur (2016–2017). UEFA Euro 2020 (Summer 2020).

Colosseum

The Colosseum in Rome is a feat of ancient engineering, and, despite its age, shares a common design with modern stadia, as well as many structural similarities.

Even today, in a world full of modern megastructures, the Colosseum is hugely impressive: a glorious but harrowing monument to Roman imperial power and cruelty. For centuries, the Romans cold-bloodedly killed thousands of people and animals on this site, in grim spectator sports watched by up to 50,000 people.

The Coliseum was primarily a venue for gladiator games.

Largest tractor

In 1977, the Big Bud 16V-747 was custom-built for the Rossi Brothers, cotton farmers in Bakersfield, California, U.S. Built built by Ron Harmon and the crew of the Northern Manufacturing Company in Havre, Montana, the tractor weighs over 45,359 kilograms! It runs on eight tyres that are each around 2.4 metres tall.

The Big Bud can work more than an acre of land per minute, at speeds up to 8 mph.

FACT FILE

Manufactured: 1977.

Number of tractors built: Just one!

Height: 4 metres.

Width: 7 metres.

Length: 8 metres.

QUEEN OF THE NETHERLANDS

The Queen of the Netherlands is a Dutch trailing suction hopper dredger ship constructed in 1998. After lengthening in 2009, she became the largest and most powerful dredger in the world. The vessel has been used in a number of high-profile salvage and dredging operations, leading to its dubious reputation as "the world's largest floating vacuum cleaner"!

FACT FILE

Manufactured: 1998.

Built by: Verolme Scheepswerf.

Owned by: Royal Boskalis Westminster.

Original length: 211 metres.

Length after modification: 230 metres.

A trailing suction hopper dredger on its way to Rotterdam port.

Komatsu D575A

The world's largest and most powerful bulldozer can move weights of up to 217,724 kilograms! The Komatsu D575A bulldozer can rip through earth and move chunks of limestone as easily you can shovel through sand. Owing to its monstrous size, the Komatsu D575A has to be dismantled and transported in seven or eight trucks!

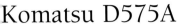

The world's largest underground machine was created to study the tiniest composition known to man: the atomic nucleus. The Large Hadron Collider is a particle accelerator housed in a 27km circular tunnel beneath the France-Switzerland border. The instrument allows scientists to crash protons together at extremely high speeds. It is hoped that these experiments will tell us more about what happened in the first moments after the Big Bang.

The Komatsu D575A is built especially for clearing large expanses of land in a short space of time.

FACT FILE

Height: 4.9 metres.

Width: 7.4 metres.

Length: 11.7 metres.

Weight: Over 130,000 kg.

31

Big Muskie

Big Muskie – the only one of its kind and size!

Big Muskie was one of the largest earthmoving machines ever built. Weighing in at over 12,200 tonnes, this megamachine stood nearly 22 stories high, and had a 330-foot twin boom and a 220-cubic yard bucket the size of a 12-car garage.

In 1976, "Big Muskie" removed 8,000 yards of overburden per operating hour for the Central Ohio Coal Co. In its 22 years of service, it removed twice the amount of earth moved during the original construction of the Panama Canal.

Shut down in 1991, "Big Muskie" was finally dismantled for scrap in 1999. Only its bucket was saved.

1978, the 13,500-tonne Bagger 288 superseded Big Muskie as the heaviest land vehicle in the world. In 1995, it was itself superseded by the slightly heavier Bagger 293 (14,200 tonnes).

After the Buran space programme was shelved, the An-225 was temporarily taken out of service.

Antonov An-225 Mriya

'Mriya' means 'dream' in Ukrainian, but the Antonov An-225 Mriya is no figment of the imagination! This strategic airlift cargo aircraft was designed by the Antonov Design Bureau in the Soviet Union in the 1980s. Powered by six turbofan engines, it is the longest and heaviest airplane ever built, with a maximum takeoff weight of 640 tonnes. It also has the largest wingspan of any aircraft in operational service.

FACT FILE

Built by: Antonov Design Bureau, Kiev, Ukraine.

Length: 84 metres.

Wingspan: 89 metres.

Engines: Six.

Cruising speed: 800-850 km/h.

First flight: December 21, 1988.

Entered service: 1989.

FACT FILE

Built by: Airbus.

Length: 73 metres.

Wingspan: 80 metres.

Can seat: 555-840 passengers.

Engines: Four.

Cruising speed: 1,014 km/h.

First test flight: April 2005.

Entered service: 2007.

A380 Super Jumbo ▼

The world's largest passenger aircraft, the Airbus A380, is one of the most environmentally advanced aircraft in the sky. With fuel efficiency as low as 3.1 litres per 100 passenger kilometres, ultra quiet engines, and a host of light-weight components, A380s fly more passengers further and more efficiently than any other large commercial aircraft. These planes are twice as long as a blue whale, and their tails are as high as five giraffes standing on top of one another!

The creators of the Airbus A380 fondly call it the 'gentle green giant' because it is cleaner, greener, quieter, and smarter than other planes.

Mil Mi-26 Halo

Designed and built by Moscow-based Mil Helicopters, the Mi-26 stands at roughly the same height as a three-story building. With rotors the same span as the wings of an Airbus A320, these megamachines are capable of transporting almost 20 tonnes of cargo, or roughly 11 family cars, at once! The Mil Mi-26 Halo is the largest and most powerful helicopter to have gone into series production.

In 1999, a Halo helicopter hauled a frozen 23,000 year-old woolly mammoth out of the Siberian tundra!

FACT FILE

Built by: MIL.

Length: 40 metres.

Height: 8.1 metres.

Engines: Two.

Cruising speed: 255 km/h.

First flight: December 14, 1977.

Entered service: 1983.

In 2015, Russian Helicopters Corp announced that they were modernising the Mi-26, to "expand the potential of this aircraft".

33

Hindenburg

Even by today's standards, the Hindenburg was huge - these airships were almost three times the size of the world's largest aircraft, Antonov An-225 Mriya!

The 245-metre Hindenburgs were passenger-carrying rigid hydrogen airships built in Germany in the 1930s. They were the last such aircraft ever built, and, in terms of their length and volume, the largest Zeppelins ever to fly. The Hindenburgs were revolutionary in their day, capable of crossing the Atlantic in just three days - twice as fast as travelling by sea.

The age of airship travel ended tragically in May 1937, when the LZ 129 Hindenburg was preparing to land at Lakehurst, New Jersey. In front of horrified onlookers, the Hindenburg exploded, and plunged to the ground in flames. Thirty-five of the 100 people on board died in the disaster.

For years the cause of the tragedy remained unknown, but in 2013 a team of experts put forward the idea that the airship had become charged with static as a result of an electrical storm. It is likely that a broken wire or sticking gas valve leaked hydrogen into the ventilation shafts so that, when ground crew members ran to take the landing ropes, they effectively "earthed" the airship, causing a spark. The fire is believed to have appeared on the zeppelin's tail, igniting the leaking hydrogen, and causing the deadly blaze.

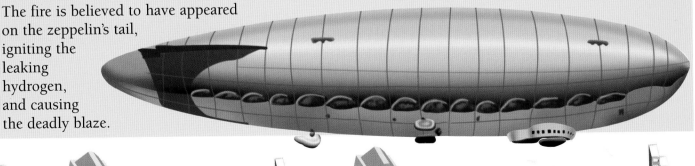

MEGA CARS

Longest Car

The longest car in the world is called the "American Dream". Designed by Jay Ohrberg of Burbank, California, U.S., the 30.5-metre limousine boasts 26 wheels, a jacuzzi, a diving board, a king-sized water bed, and even a helicopter landing pad! In 2014, New York's Autoseum Automotive Teaching Museum announced that they had acquired the car, which had been abandoned in a New Jersey warehouse and was in dire need of repair. These days it is being used to help teach students to fix, build and fabricate cars.

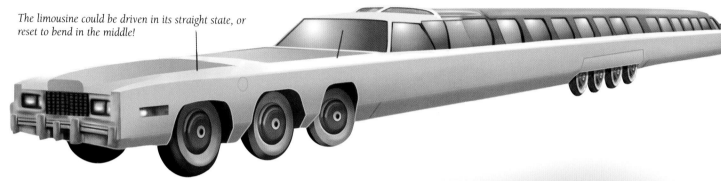

The limousine could be driven in its straight state, or reset to bend in the middle!

Bigfoot

Bob Chandler of St Louis, U.S., loves building monster trucks! His Bigfoot trucks are a regular feature of monster truck races. A former construction worker from the St. Louis, Missouri area, Chandler began building the first Bigfoot in 1975, using his family's 1974 Ford F-250 four-wheel-drive. When, in 1981, Chandler obtained permission from a local farmer to place two dilapidated cars in his field and crush them with Bigfoot, he not only changed his life and fortune, but also the future of motorsports. Car-crushing and monster truck racing became popular spectator sports the world over. In 2012, the Bigfoot team took a huge leap forward in technology and innovation when BIGFOOT #20 was completed. It is the world's first and only battery-powered monster truck!

The Bigfoot 5 is the largest of all monster trucks

Tallest Rideable Motorbike

The tallest rideable motorcycle measures 5.10 metres from the ground to the top of the handlebars. It was constructed by Italian Fabio Reggiani, and was was ridden over a 100m course at Montecchio Emilia on 24 March 2012.

The world's largest bus is almost 31 metres long and can carry 256 passengers! The AutoTram Extra Grand was trialled in Dresden, Germany in 2012.

FACT FILE

Built: 2012

Built by: Fabio Reggiani.

Height: 5.1 metres.

Weight: 2498 kg.

Height of tyres: 1.88 metres.

World's Longest Motorbike

Measuring an incredible 22 metres long, the world's longest motorbike (which is, in fact, a converted 125cc scooter!) took a month build and can carry up to 25 people on board!

Colin Furze built the vehicle in an attempt to gain another Guinness World Record - he already holds the record for the fastest mobility scooter, with a top speed of 71mph!

To set the record he took the behemoth to the Saltby Airfield in Granthan and rode it for a mile along the runway hitting a top speed of 35mph.

Colin Furze also holds the record for the world's fastest mobility scooter!

Image licensed by Ingram Image.

The Yamato *played a key role for the Imperial Japanese Navy during World War II*

Mega battleships

They were the largest battleships ever built. Constructed at Kure, Japan, both *Yamato* and *Musashi* played vital roles in the Japanese Navy during World War II. On 24th October 24, 1944, while *Musashi* was on its way to the Leyte landing beach, it was attacked by U.S. Navy aircraft. She sank during the Battle of the Sibuyan Sea, taking 17 bomb and 19 torpedo hits, with the loss of 1,023 of her 2,399-man crew.

The *Yamato* set sail for the last time in April 1945. The ship was a part of Operation Ten-Go and had been despatched to attack the American fleet. It was hit by around 20 bombs and torpedoes before the ship's ammunitions blew up – sinking it in the process. Tragically, 2,498 of the 2,700 crew-members were lost in the disaster.

36

USS Ronald Reagan

The ninth ship in the Nimitz-class aircraft carriers, USS *Ronald Reagan*, is one of the few U.S. naval ships to be named after a living person. It is a nuclear-powered vessel, capable of accommodating 6,000 naval staff and more than 80 warplanes. The ship's two nuclear reactors can propel the ship for more than 20 years without refuelling!

At over 1,090 feet, the USS Ronald Reagan is almost as long as the Empire State Building is tall! She can carry enough food to serve up to 18,150 meals every day for three months!

Queen Mary 2

RMS *Queen Mary 2* is the flagship of the Cunard Line, a famous British cruise line. Among its many facilitites, the largest passenger ship ever to sail the oceans boasts the largest dancefloor and the first planetarium at sea, a luxury 3D cinema, a theatre, a casino, five swimming pools, and fifteen restaurants and bars. At 345 metres long, the Queen Mary 2 is the length of four football pitches, and the same height as a 23-storey building.

Queen Mary 2 is the flagship of the Cunard Line.

In 2015, 70 years after the sinking of the Musashi, researchers found a sprawling undersea wreck at the bottom of the Philippines' Sibuyan Sea. It was the culmination of an eight-year search for the lost battleship.

FACT FILE

Length: 345 metres.

Weight: 76,000 tonnes (empty).

Construction began: July 4, 2002.

Launched: September 25, 2003.

Maiden voyage: January 12, 2004 Southampton, England, to Fort Lauderdale, Florida, U.S.

MONT

Seawise Giant, later Happy Giant, Jahre Viking, Knock Nevis, Oppama, and finally, Mont, was an Ultra Large Crude Carrier Supertanker and the longest ship ever built. She was sunk during the Iran–Iraq War, but was later salvaged and restored to service.

Last used as a floating storage and offloading unit (FSO) moored off the coast of Qatar in the Persian Gulf, the vessel was eventually sold to Indian ship breakers, and renamed Mont for her final journey in December 2009. After clearing Indian customs, she was sailed to, and intentionally beached at, Alang, Gujarat, India, to be broken up for scrap.

Before its decommission, Mont was the longest ship ever built.

The Ghan

The Ghan is comfortably the world's longest passenger train, with its sister train in Australia, the Indian Pacific, the next longest at 774 metres. Consisting of 44 carriages and two locomotives, The Ghan is the combined length of 12 football pitches! It travels at an average speed of 85 kilometres per hour, with a top speed of 115 kilometres per hour.

FACT FILE

Operated by:
Great Southern Rail.

Service began: 1912.

Locomotives: diesel-electric
locomotives.

Max speed: 115 km/h.

38

BHP Freight Train

BHP Iron Ore set a new world record, running the longest and heaviest freight train in 2001.

On 21 June, 2001, BHP Iron Ore set a new world record, running the longest and heaviest freight train between Yandi mine and Port Hedland in the Pilbara region of Western Australia. Carrying some 82,000 wet tonnes of iron ore, the 7.3 kilometre train was formed of 682 wagons hauled by all eight of BHPIO's General Electric AC6000CW diesel locomotives. The gross weight of the vehcile was an astonishing 99,734 tonnes! BHP already held the record for the heaviest train prior to this, with a 10-loco 540-wagon special on 28th May 1996, with a gross weight of 72,191 tonnes.

FACT FILE

Operated by: BHP Billiton
Iron Ore, Australia.

Length: 7.3 kilometres.

Weight: 99,732 tonnes.

Locomotives: Eight diesel-
electric locomotives.

Of the 25 Big Boys, eight have been preserved.

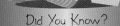

FACT FILE

Operated by:
Union Pacific Railroad, U.S.

Built by:
American Locomotive Company, U.S.

Length:
40.5 m (133 feet).

Weight:
540 tonnes.

Top speed: 130 km/hour.

Big Boy

The American Locomotive Co. in Schenectady, N.Y., built 25 Big Boy locomotives to Union Pacific's specifications between 1941 and 1944. The monstrous trains became legendary. They were the largest steam locomotives ever to work the rugged terrain of the American West. Of the 25 Big Boy locomotives manufactured, today only eight remain. Seven are on static display, and one is undergoing a restoration to operating condition for excursion service.

Trans-Siberian Railway

The longest railway track in the world, the Trans-Siberian Railway stretches across two continents and spans a record seven time zones! The 9,289 km railway has connected Moscow with Vladivostok since 1916, and is still be expanded today. Construction began in 1891 under the supervision of government ministers who were personally appointed by Tsar Alexander III and his son, Tsar Nicholas II.

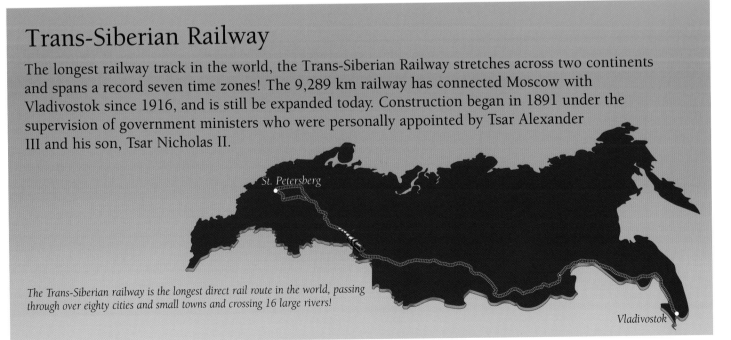

The Trans-Siberian railway is the longest direct rail route in the world, passing through over eighty cities and small towns and crossing 16 large rivers!

St. Petersberg

Vladivostok

MORE MEGA WONDERS

TAJ MAHAL

The Taj Mahal is one of the most recognised buildings in the world, and arguably one of the most beautiful.

This giant mausoleum of white marble is situated on the south bank of the Yamuna river, in the Indian city of Agra. It was built between 1632 and 1653 by order of the Mughal emperor Shah Jahan, in memory of his favourite wife, Mumtaz Mahal, a persian princess who died giving birth to their 14th child. The most spectacular feature of the Taj Mahal is the marble dome that surmounts Mahal's tomb. It stands 35 metres tall, and is decorated with a lotus design.

"Taj Mahal" means "Crown Palaces" in persian. In 2007 it was declared a winner of the New7Wonders the World initiative.

Image licensed by Ingram Image.

40

London Eye

At 135 metres high, the London Eye is the world's largest cantilevered observation wheel. Like the Millennium Dome, it was built as part of England's Millennium Project, but was received with far more enthusiasm than the ill-fated Dome (which was beset with financial problems). Originally intended as a temporary structure, able to be dismantled and transported to a new location, the Eye had planning permission for just five years. But its enduring popularity with visitors led to the Eye becoming a permanent fixture on the London skyline: an iconic symbol of the modern city.

Like the Millennium Dome, the London Eye was a part of England's Millennium Project.

The Medusa ride at Six Flags boasts the world's ONLY sea serpent roll.

When riding Full Throttle, the steel roller coaster at Six Flags Magic Mountain in Valencia, California, riders experience the world's tallest loop at 38.75 metres.

The entire ride lasts a hair-raising 1 minute 30 seconds!

Six Flags Magic Mountain

Six Flags Magic Mountain is a 262-acre theme park in the Valencia neighborhood of Santa Clarita, California, north of Los Angeles. With 19 roller coasters, the park holds the world record for the most roller coasters in an amusement park.

FACT FILE

Location:
Valencia, California, United States.

First roller coaster:
Gold Rusher, 1971.

Number of visitors:
3,104,000 in 2015.

Fastest roller coaster:
Kingda Ka
(second fastest in the world).

Smithsonian Museum

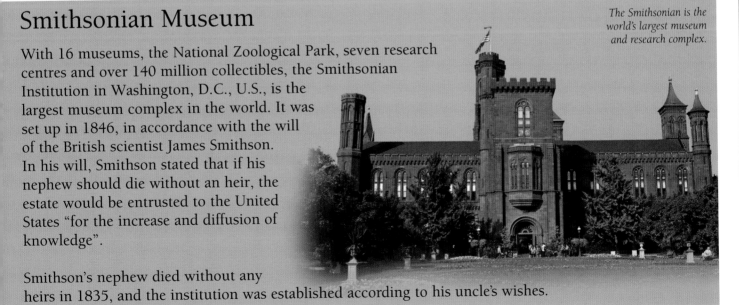

The Smithsonian is the world's largest museum and research complex.

With 16 museums, the National Zoological Park, seven research centres and over 140 million collectibles, the Smithsonian Institution in Washington, D.C., U.S., is the largest museum complex in the world. It was set up in 1846, in accordance with the will of the British scientist James Smithson. In his will, Smithson stated that if his nephew should die without an heir, the estate would be entrusted to the United States "for the increase and diffusion of knowledge".

Smithson's nephew died without any heirs in 1835, and the institution was established according to his uncle's wishes.

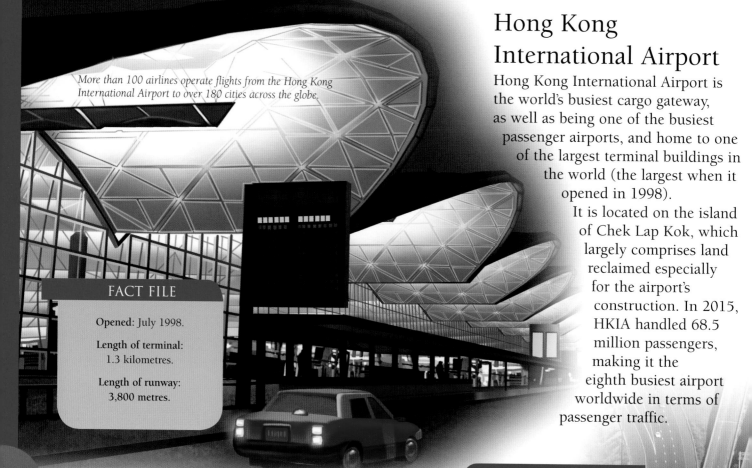

More than 100 airlines operate flights from the Hong Kong International Airport to over 180 cities across the globe.

FACT FILE

Opened: July 1998.

Length of terminal:
1.3 kilometres.

Length of runway:
3,800 metres.

42

Hong Kong International Airport

Hong Kong International Airport is the world's busiest cargo gateway, as well as being one of the busiest passenger airports, and home to one of the largest terminal buildings in the world (the largest when it opened in 1998).

It is located on the island of Chek Lap Kok, which largely comprises land reclaimed especially for the airport's construction. In 2015, HKIA handled 68.5 million passengers, making it the eighth busiest airport worldwide in terms of passenger traffic.

U.S. Interstate Highway

Inspired by the network of high-speed roads he saw in Germany during World War II, Dwight D. Eisenhower championed the passing of the Federal-Aid Highway Act of 1956. This law funded the first 41,000 miles of the early U.S. interstate system, which now boasts 46,876 miles and runs through all 50 states!

FACT FILE

• It took 17 years to create and fund the interstate. Although the idea was first put forward in 1939, it wasn't until the Act of 1956 that funding was finally allocated to its construction.

• Every state owns its own section, and is responsible for its maintenance and law enforcement.

• The red, white, and blue shields used to designate interstate numbers are trademarked by the American Association of State Highway Officials!

Image licensed by Ingram Image.

43

The Autobahn speed record was set on January 8th, 1938, and has never been broken! Rudolf Caracciola, a Formula One racer, set the 268.9mph record in a Mercedes-Benz W125 with a V-12 engine. His rival, Bernd Rosemeyer, was killed competing for the record on the same day.

FACT FILE

Total length:
Over 12,000 kilometres.

First section opened: 1935.

Width of lanes: 3.75 metres.

Speed limit: 1130 km/h.

Autobahn

While the idea behind the Autobahn emerged in the 1920s, full-scale construction didn't get underway until Hitler came to power in 1933. By 1936 he had 130,000 people building one of the world's first high-speed roads. The inaugural section opened in 1935, stretching from Frankfurt am Main to Darmstadt. Today, Germany's autobahn network has a total length of around 12,949 kilometres, ranking it among the most dense and longest raod systems in the world. Longer systems can be found in China (111,950 kilometres), the United States (77,017 kilometres), and Spain (16,583 kilometres).

Suez Canal

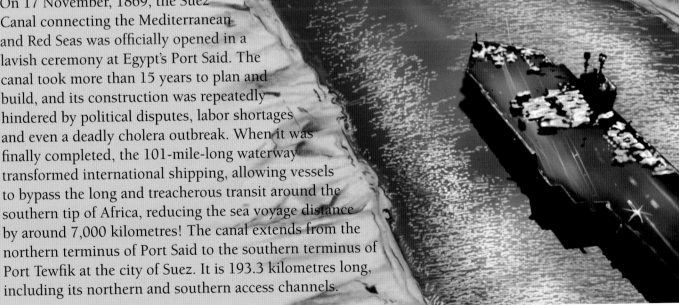

On 17 November, 1869, the Suez Canal connecting the Mediterranean and Red Seas was officially opened in a lavish ceremony at Egypt's Port Said. The canal took more than 15 years to plan and build, and its construction was repeatedly hindered by political disputes, labor shortages and even a deadly cholera outbreak. When it was finally completed, the 101-mile-long waterway transformed international shipping, allowing vessels to bypass the long and treacherous transit around the southern tip of Africa, reducing the sea voyage distance by around 7,000 kilometres! The canal extends from the northern terminus of Port Said to the southern terminus of Port Tewfik at the city of Suez. It is 193.3 kilometres long, including its northern and southern access channels.

The modern Suez Canal is only the most recent of several manmade waterways that once snaked their way across Egypt. The Egyptian Pharaoh Senusret III may have built an early canal connecting the Red Sea and the Nile River around 1850 B.C.

FUTURE MEGASTRUCTURES

The landscape around us is constantly evolving as advances in technology mean that we are able to build more ambitious structures faster and more safely than ever before.

World records are constantly being broken, with yesterday's marvels being knocked off the top spots by the megastructures of today.

The inspiration for the i360 came from architects David Marks and Julia Barfield, the husband and wife team, who famously designed the London Eye.

FACT FILE

Location: Brighton, England.

Height: 161 metres.

Construction started: 2014.

Completed: Summer 2016.

44

BRITISH AIRWAYS i360

As this title goes to print, the town of Brighton in England is celebrating the opening of the world's thinnest tall building. Visitors to the 161 metre British Airways i360 viewing tower ascend 137 metres in a 360-degree curved-glass pod, where they can enjoy views from Bexhill in East Sussex to Chichester in West Sussex, and the South Downs to the north.

But what does the future hold for the world of Megastructure engineering?

JEDDAH TOWER

The title of world's tallest building is likely to be snatched from Dubai's Burj Khalifa in 2020 by Saudi Arabia's Jeddah Tower, which is set to become the first structure ever to reach the one-kilometre high mark!

The Kingdom Tower, as it is also known, will have 200 floors, housing the world's highest observatory, a 200-room Four Seasons Hotel, 121 serviced apartments, 260 residential apartments, and corporate offices.

FACT FILE

Names: Jeddah Tower; Kingdom Tower; Mile-High Tower.

Status: Under construction.

Location: Jeddah, Saudi Arabia.

Floor area: 245,000 square metres.

Construction began: April 2013.

Estimated completion: 2020.

LONDON BRIDGES

Meanwhile, in London, plans are being drawn up for the construction of no fewer than 13 new bridges and tunnels along the River Thames. It is believed that these new structures would not only improve day-to-day travelling throughout England's capital city, but also unlock areas of development, creating thousands of new jobs and homes.

Image licensed by Ingram Image.

ROAD STRADDLING BUS

China is developing an altogether more creative way of easing everyday travelling, however. Wasting time in traffic jams could become a thing of the past with the development of the world's first road-straddling bus! The giant Transit Explore Bus, which itself looks like a motorised bridge, is 21 metres long and over seven metres wide. Each TEB can transport hundreds of passengers at any one time, and up to four vehicles can be linked together, replacing up to 40 conventional buses!

These futuristic-looking vehicles are powered by electricity, and can travel at up to 60km/h. They run on tracks with passenger spaces standing two metres above the road, so that two lanes of traffic can pass undisturbed beneath them.

It is unclear when the buses will be used in Chinese cities, but they will no doubt help to ease the notorious traffic jams of the country's biggest cities if they are eventually put in to mass production.

One TEB could replace up to 10 conventional buses.

Image licensed by Ingram Image.